Love Is

Hannah Walton

Cover Art by Taylor Perkey

From the *ESV*® Bible (*The Holy Bible, English Standard Version*®), copyright 2001 by Crossway, a publishing ministry of Good News Publishers. Used by permission. All rights reserved.

All rights reserved. No part of this publication may be reproduced, stored in a retrieval system, or transmitted in any form, or by any means – electronic, mechanical, photocopying, recording or otherwise – without the prior permission of the author. The only exception is brief quotation in printed reviews.

For more information contact:

Hannah Walton

hannahb_walton@yahoo.com

Introduction

I remember one night during my first semester of college, I was sitting in my car, praying and asking God to help me understand. I had a broken heart and I was feeling lost. "I just need to know that Your kind of love exists here. I'm tired of the world's interpretation." World love fails, it does not satisfy, and quite honestly, it has been twisted around to fit our emotions and conveniences. Quite frankly, it's more like lust. In a world where Christians are supposed to be recognized by their love (John 13:35), we've missed it and become known for our judgment and inconsistency. I finally got sick of it and decided to ask God to teach me to love His way. So, I did. His answer took me by surprise. He started to show me things I had never seen before, and He gave me a new perspective. He took me back to the familiar 1 Corinthians 13 passage. I know we hear it all the time, and I'll be the first to admit it started to sound monotonous to me, but this time felt like I was reading it for the first time. The Holy Spirit completely rocked my world by putting it in a new light.

A lot of my frustration came from the fact that I wasn't getting this kind of love from the people around me, especially other Christians. However, as I was reading it again, I realized that I wasn't giving that kind of love either. How can I expect someone to be patient with me if I'm not patient with them? That got me. I decided I needed to get serious about practicing heaven's kind of love if I ever wanted to receive it. After all, you reap what you sow.

Next, the Lord started giving me ideas. He is so good about opening the door whenever we knock. The following thirteen weeks of my life were anything but easy, but I can say with confidence that they held some of the absolute best experiences of my life. I did exactly what you are about to do. Each week I practiced one of the thirteen attributes of love mentioned in 1 Corinthians 13. It was a lot of praying and fasting, saturating myself in the Word, and checking myself. I even wrote the words on my arm to remind myself to be intentional throughout the day. Being intentional about applying the Scriptures to your life is powerful, and the daily surrender gives God room to move, repair, and refresh.

I will tell you from the start, this will be challenging, but I cannot stress to you enough how worth it, it is. You will get out of it as much as you put in, so decide how much you are willing to give. The more you let go of, the more space Jesus has to come fill and bless you.

This experience changed my life and formed habits that are now a part of my day-to-day living. I have grown leaps and bounds, built friendships with some of the most genuine and incredible people I have ever met, and now have a closer relationship with Jesus. And it keeps getting better!

I encourage you to walk this journey with someone. It always helps to have accountability and support to keep going through the hard parts. Find a friend or a group of friends and pray for each other. Check on each other and discuss the things God is showing you. It builds faith and strong relationships. The first time I did this, my friend Megan joined me. I asked her if she would let me include part of her experience and this is what she had to say:

> When Hannah and I first decided to start this life-altering challenge in her car one Sunday night, I had no idea how stretching it would be. The first week when we had to be patient, I can't tell you how happy I was that it was over. That was until Hannah brought up the idea of having the weeks build on one another and I realized I had to be patient for thirteen weeks. Ugh! At first it was hard, but by the end it was a joy. I had no problem sitting in traffic or waiting on money to come in for things I needed.
>
> This was one of the most humbling things I have ever done. Hannah and I prayed with each other every night during those thirteen weeks and it built up endurance, faith, and friendship. I learned to have a teachable spirit, to embrace messy days along the

way, and what it really means to be the example of love. I often go back and do this challenge again because I grew so much. I have no doubt that you will too.

Like Megan mentioned, each week builds. When you finish one week, don't just forget about it. Continue to practice the characteristics you have already covered so you begin to form habits.

Again, it will not be easy, but it will be worth it. It will stretch you, and by the end, you won't believe how much you have grown! There is also a challenge for each week to help you put your applications into action. Although the challenge is explained on a specific day, feel free to do it any time during the week.

I pray that during the next thirteen weeks you would learn to trust God with everything you have, allow Him to come and transform your heart, and renew your mind, and discover the love that never fails.

Since writing this book, I have gone back and done this study over again. Let me tell you, it gets better every time. The Lord has continued to teach me new things about love, one of which being the reason this process is so important. It was my second time through the study, and I asked God about the end of 1 Corinthians 13, "So now faith, hope, and love abide, these three; but the greatest of these is love." I asked Him why love is the greatest, not in disagreement, but out of curiosity. I figured faith was pretty important, too. Immediately the verse in 1 John 4 came to mind: "Anyone who does not love does not know God, because God is love." It hit me then. Of course! Love is the most important because God *is* Love. Because of Him, we have faith and hope. Then I went back to 1 Corinthians and read it like this: God is patient and kind; God does not envy or boast; God is not arrogant or rude. God does not insist on His own way. He is not irritable or resentful. He does not rejoice at wrongdoing, but rejoices with the truth. God bears all things. God believes all things. God hopes all things, and God endures all things.

Once I realized this, it completely changed my perspective. As I was practicing these characteristics, I was practicing being like Him. When we are learning about love, we are actually learning about who God is. Whenever we apply these Scriptures to our lives and put our faith into action, sharing this love with the world around us, we are displaying the heart of God. I think that's pretty cool.

I believe that as you go through these pages and make this your story, the Lord will reveal Himself to you in ways you never imagined. He will show you things you never realized before, and take you on a journey that will change you forever. So, open your Bible to 1 Corinthians 13, and let's get started!

Before we begin...

Write down what you hope to see happen during the next thirteen weeks.

_____
_____
_____
_____
_____
_____
_____
_____
_____
_____
_____
_____
_____
_____
_____
_____
_____
_____
_____
_____
_____
_____
_____
_____
_____

DAY 1

Love is…

Patient

"Better is the end of a thing than its beginning, and the patient in spirit is better than the proud in spirit." Ecclesiastes 7:8

What is patience?

Write down what patience means in your own words, look up the definition, and read 1 Corinthians 13 in several different versions to get a good idea of what you're going to be dealing with this week.

_____
_____
_____
_____
_____
_____
_____
_____
_____
_____
_____
_____
_____
_____
_____
_____
_____

DAY 2

Love is…

Patient

"But if we hope for what we do not see, we wait for it with patience."

Romans 8:25

Why is patience important in regards to love?

_____
_____
_____
_____
_____
_____
_____
_____
_____
_____
_____
_____
_____
_____
_____
_____
_____
_____

DAY 3

Love is…

Patient

"May you be strengthened with all power, according to his glorious might, for all endurance and patience with joy." Colossians 1:11

Apply it.

Whom can you be patient with today, and how?

_____
_____
_____
_____
_____
_____
_____
_____
_____
_____
_____
_____
_____
_____
_____
_____

DAY 4

Love is…

Patient

"And count the patience of our Lord as salvation…" 2 Peter 3:15

Spend some time in prayer.

Ask God to give you opportunities to work on being patient and to help you be aware when those times come, so you can be intentional. Write down anything that comes to mind.

_____
_____
_____
_____
_____
_____
_____
_____
_____
_____
_____
_____
_____
_____
_____
_____
_____
_____

DAY 5

Love is…

Patient

"As an example of suffering and patience, brothers, take the prophets who spoke in the name of the Lord. Behold, we consider those blessed who remain steadfast. You have heard of the steadfastness of Job, and you have seen the purpose of the Lord, how the Lord is compassionate and merciful." James 5:10-11

Take some time to look up verses about patience. Write them below, and then pick one or two to put on a notecard. Take them with you today, and read or say them whenever you get a chance.

_____
_____
_____
_____
_____
_____
_____
_____
_____
_____
_____
_____

DAY 6

Love is…

Patient

"But I received mercy for this reason, that in me, as the foremost, Jesus Christ might display his perfect patience as an example to those who were to believe in him for eternal life." 1 Timothy 1:16

Challenge:

Go somewhere and wait in the longest line. If someone gets in line behind you, let them go first. Do this until it no longer bothers you to wait. Write about your experience below.

_____
_____
_____
_____
_____
_____
_____
_____
_____
_____
_____
_____
_____
_____
_____

DAY 7

Love is…

Patient

"Put on then, as God's chosen ones, holy and beloved, compassionate hearts, kindness, humility, meekness, and patience, bearing with one another and, if one has a complaint against another, forgiving each other; as the Lord has forgiven you, so you must also forgive."
Colossians 3:12-13

Reflect.

What have you learned while practicing patience?

_____
_____
_____
_____
_____
_____
_____
_____
_____
_____
_____
_____
_____

DAY 8

Love is…

Kind

"A man who is kind benefits himself, but a cruel man hurts himself."
Proverbs 11:17

What is kindness?

Write down what kindness means in your own words, look up the definition, and read 1 Corinthians 13 in several different versions to get a good idea of what you're going to be dealing with this week.

_____
_____
_____
_____
_____
_____
_____
_____
_____
_____
_____
_____
_____
_____
_____
_____

DAY 9

Love is…

Kind

"Gracious words are like a honeycomb, sweetness to the soul and health to the body." Proverbs 16:24

Why is kindness important in regards to love?

_____
_____
_____
_____
_____
_____
_____
_____
_____
_____
_____
_____
_____
_____
_____
_____
_____
_____

DAY 10

Love is…

Kind

"Whoever pursues righteousness and kindness will find life, righteousness, and honor." Proverbs 21:21

Apply it.

Whom can you be kind to today, and how?

DAY 11

Love is…

Kind

"The Lord is righteous in all his ways and kind in all his works."

Psalm 145:17

Spend some time in prayer.

Ask God to give you opportunities to work on being kind and to help you be aware when those times come, so you can be intentional. Write down anything that comes to mind.

_____
_____
_____
_____
_____
_____
_____
_____
_____
_____
_____
_____
_____
_____
_____
_____

DAY 12

Love is…

Kind

"Be kind to one another, tenderhearted, forgiving one another, as God in Christ forgave you." Ephesians 4:32

Take some time to look up verses about kindness. Write them below, and then pick one or two to put on a notecard. Take them with you today, and read or say them whenever you get a chance.

_____
_____
_____
_____
_____
_____
_____
_____
_____
_____
_____
_____
_____
_____
_____
_____

DAY 13

Love is…

Kind

"He who withholds kindness from a friend forsakes the fear of the Almighty." Job 6:14

Challenge:

Go out of your way to be kind to someone. Write a note, pay for a meal, offer a smile. Write about your experience below.

_____
_____
_____
_____
_____
_____
_____
_____
_____
_____
_____
_____
_____
_____
_____

DAY 14

Love is…

Kind

"Note then the kindness and the severity of God: severity toward those who have fallen, but God's kindness to you, provided you continue in his kindness. Otherwise you too will be cut off." Romans 11:22

Reflect.

What have you learned while practicing kindness?

_____
_____
_____
_____
_____
_____
_____
_____
_____
_____
_____
_____
_____
_____
_____
_____

DAY 15

Love is…

Not Envious

"A tranquil heart gives life to the flesh, but envy makes the bones rot."
Proverbs 14:30

What is envy?

Write down what being envious means in your own words, look up the definition, and read 1 Corinthians 13 in several different versions to get a good idea of what you're going to be dealing with this week.

_____
_____
_____
_____
_____
_____
_____
_____
_____
_____
_____
_____
_____
_____
_____
_____

DAY 16

Love is…

Not Envious

"For where jealousy and selfish ambition exist, there will be disorder and every vile practice." James 3:16

Why is not being envious important in regards to love?

_____
_____
_____
_____
_____
_____
_____
_____
_____
_____
_____
_____
_____
_____
_____
_____
_____
_____
_____

DAY 17

Love is...

Not Envious

"Wrath is cruel, anger is overwhelming, but who can stand before jealousy?" Proverbs 27:4

Apply it.

How can you work on not being envious today?

_____
_____
_____
_____
_____
_____
_____
_____
_____
_____
_____
_____
_____
_____
_____
_____
_____
_____

DAY 18

Love is…

Not Envious

"Let us not become conceited, provoking one another, envying one another." Galatians 5:26

Spend some time in prayer.

Ask God to give you opportunities to work on not being envious and to help you be aware when those times come, so you can be intentional. Write down anything that comes to mind.

_____
_____
_____
_____
_____
_____
_____
_____
_____
_____
_____
_____
_____
_____
_____
_____
_____

DAY 19

Love is...

Not Envious

"Some indeed preach Christ from envy and rivalry, but others from good will." Philippians 1:15

Take some time to look up verses about envy. Write them below, and then pick one or two to put on a notecard. Take them with you today, and read or say them whenever you get a chance.

_____
_____
_____
_____
_____
_____
_____
_____
_____
_____
_____
_____
_____
_____
_____
_____
_____

DAY 20

Love is…

Not Envious

"But if you have bitter jealousy and selfish ambition in your hearts, do not boast and be false to the truth." James 3:14

Challenge:

Remember that God doesn't see any one of us as better than another. When you find yourself wishing you had what someone else has or comparing yourself to others, don't let jealousy get the best of you. Give a genuine compliment instead. Write about your experience below.

_____
_____
_____
_____
_____
_____
_____
_____
_____
_____
_____
_____
_____

DAY 21

Love is…

Not Envious

"Surely vexation kills the fool, and jealousy slays the simple." Job 5:2

Reflect.

What have you learned while practicing not being envious?

_____
_____
_____
_____
_____
_____
_____
_____
_____
_____
_____
_____
_____
_____
_____
_____
_____
_____
_____
_____

DAY 22

Love is…

Not Boastful or Arrogant

"Let the one who boasts, boast in the Lord." 2 Corinthians 10:17

What are boasting and arrogance?

Write down what being boastful or arrogant means in your own words, look up the definition, and read 1 Corinthians 13 in several different versions to get a good idea of what you're going to be dealing with this week.

_____
_____
_____
_____
_____
_____
_____
_____
_____
_____
_____
_____
_____
_____
_____
_____
_____

DAY 23

Love is…

Not Boastful or Arrogant

"When pride comes, then comes disgrace, but with the humble is wisdom." Proverbs 11:2

Why is not being boastful or arrogant important in regards to love?

_____
_____
_____
_____
_____
_____
_____
_____
_____
_____
_____
_____
_____
_____
_____
_____
_____
_____
_____

DAY 24

Love is…

Not Boastful or Arrogant

"For by grace you have been saved through faith. And this is not your own doing; it is the gift of God, not a result of works, so that no one may boast." Ephesians 2:8-9

Apply it.

How can you work on not being boastful or arrogant today?

_____
_____
_____
_____
_____
_____
_____
_____
_____
_____
_____
_____
_____
_____
_____
_____
_____

DAY 25

Love is…

Not Boastful or Arrogant

"For all that is in the world – the desires of the flesh and the desires of the eyes and pride of life – is not from the Father but is from the world." 1 John 2:16

Spend some time in prayer.

Ask God to give you opportunities to work on not being boastful or arrogant and to help you be aware when those times come, so you can be intentional. Write down anything that comes to mind.

_____
_____
_____
_____
_____
_____
_____
_____
_____
_____
_____
_____
_____
_____
_____
_____

DAY 26

Love is…

Not Boastful or Arrogant

"But we will not boast beyond limits, but will boast only with regard to the area of influence God assigned to us, to reach even to you."

2 Corinthians 10:13

Take some time to look up verses about being boastful or arrogant. Write them below, and then pick one or two to put on a notecard. Take them with you today, and read or say them whenever you get a chance.

_____
_____
_____
_____
_____
_____
_____
_____
_____
_____
_____
_____
_____
_____
_____
_____

DAY 27

Love is…

Not Boastful or Arrogant

"By insolence comes nothing but strife, but with those who take advice is wisdom." Proverbs 13:10

Challenge:

Try not to talk about yourself or your accomplishments for a day. Focus on encouraging, supporting and listening to others. Write about your experience below.

_____
_____
_____
_____
_____
_____
_____
_____
_____
_____
_____
_____
_____
_____
_____
_____

DAY 28

Love is…

Not Boastful or Arrogant

"Pride goes before destruction, and a haughty spirit before a fall."
Proverbs 16:18

Reflect.

What have you learned while practicing not being boastful or arrogant?

_____
_____
_____
_____
_____
_____
_____
_____
_____
_____
_____
_____
_____
_____
_____
_____

DAY 29

Love is…

Not Rude

"Do nothing from selfish ambition or conceit, but in humility count others more significant than yourselves." Philippians 2:3

What is being rude?

Write down what being rude means in your own words, look up the definition, and read 1 Corinthians 13 in several different versions to get a good idea of what you're going to be dealing with this week.

_____
_____
_____
_____
_____
_____
_____
_____
_____
_____
_____
_____
_____
_____
_____
_____
_____

DAY 30

Love is…

Not Rude

"Be kind to one another, tenderhearted, forgiving one another, as God in Christ forgave you." Ephesians 4:32

Why is not being rude important in regards to love?

_____
_____
_____
_____
_____
_____
_____
_____
_____
_____
_____
_____
_____
_____
_____
_____
_____

DAY 31

Love is…

Not Rude

"Love one another with brotherly affection. Outdo one another in showing honor." Romans 12:10

Apply it.

How can you work on not being rude today?

_____
_____
_____
_____
_____
_____
_____
_____
_____
_____
_____
_____
_____
_____
_____
_____
_____
_____
_____

DAY 32

Love is…

Not Rude

"A gentle tongue is a tree of life, but perverseness in it breaks the spirit." Proverbs 15:4

Spend some time in prayer.

Ask God to give you opportunities to work on not being rude and to help you be aware when those times come, so you can be intentional. Write down anything that comes to mind.

_____
_____
_____
_____
_____
_____
_____
_____
_____
_____
_____
_____
_____
_____
_____
_____

DAY 33

Love is…

Not Rude

"Therefore you have no excuse, O man, every one of you who judges. For in passing judgment on another you condemn yourself, because you, the judge, practice the very same things." Romans 2:1

Take some time to look up verses about being rude. Write them below, and then pick one or two to put on a notecard. Take them with you today, and read or say them whenever you get a chance.

_____
_____
_____
_____
_____
_____
_____
_____
_____
_____
_____
_____
_____
_____
_____
_____
_____

DAY 34

Love is…

Not Rude

"Let no corrupting talk come out of your mouths, but only such as is good for building up, as fits the occasion, that it may give grace to those who hear." Ephesians 4:29

Challenge:

Don't gossip. Resist the urge to talk rudely about that waitress, coworker, friend, etc. Instead, build people up today. Write about your experience below.

_____
_____
_____
_____
_____
_____
_____
_____
_____
_____
_____
_____
_____
_____
_____

DAY 35

Love is…

Not Rude

"Let your speech always be gracious, seasoned with salt, so that you may know how you ought to answer each person." Colossians 4:6

Reflect.

What have you learned while practicing not being rude?

___
___
___
___
___
___
___
___
___
___
___
___
___
___
___
___
___
___
___

DAY 36

Love is…

Not Insistent on Its Own Way

"It shall not be so among you. But whoever would be great among you must be your servant, and whoever would be first among you must be your slave, even as the Son of Man came not to be served but to serve, and to give his life as a ransom for many." Matthew 20:26-28

What is not insisting your own way?

Write down what not insisting on its own way means in your own words, look up the definition of insisting, and read 1 Corinthians 13 in several different versions to get a good idea of what you're going to be dealing with this week.

DAY 37

Love is…

Not Insistent on Its Own Way

"Give to the one who begs from you, and do not refuse the one who would borrow from you." Matthew 5:42

Why is not insisting on your own way important in regards to love?

_____
_____
_____
_____
_____
_____
_____
_____
_____
_____
_____
_____
_____
_____
_____
_____
_____
_____
_____
_____

DAY 38

Love is…

Not Insistent on Its Own Way

"In all things I have shown you that by working hard in this way we must help the weak and remember the words of the Lord Jesus, how he himself said, 'It is more blessed to give than to receive.'" Acts 20:35

Apply it.

How can you work on not insisting on your own way today?

_____
_____
_____
_____
_____
_____
_____
_____
_____
_____
_____
_____
_____
_____
_____
_____
_____

DAY 39

Love is…

Not Insistent on Its Own Way

"Let each of you look not only to his own interests, but also to the interests of others." Philippians 2:4

Spend some time in prayer.

Ask God to give you opportunities to work on not insisting on your own way and to help you be aware when those times come, so you can be intentional. Write down anything that comes to mind.

_____
_____
_____
_____
_____
_____
_____
_____
_____
_____
_____
_____
_____
_____
_____
_____

DAY 40

Love is…

Not Insistent on Its Own Way

"And the King will answer them, 'Truly, I say to you, as you did it to one of the least of these my brothers, you did it to me.'" Matthew 25:40

Take some time to look up verses about not insisting on your own way based on the definitions you found earlier in the week. Write them below, and then pick one or two to put on a notecard. Take them with you today, and read or say them whenever you get a chance.

_____
_____
_____
_____
_____
_____
_____
_____
_____
_____
_____
_____
_____
_____
_____
_____
_____

DAY 41

Love is…

Not Insistent on Its Own Way

"Bear one another's burdens, and so fulfill the law of Christ. For if anyone thinks he is something, when he is nothing, he deceives himself." Galatians 6:2-3

Challenge:

Do what someone else wants to do, without complaining. Write about your experience below.

_____
_____
_____
_____
_____
_____
_____
_____
_____
_____
_____
_____
_____
_____
_____
_____

DAY 42

Love is…

Not Insistent on Its Own Way

"As you wish that others would do to you, do so to them." Luke 6:31

Reflect.

What have you learned while practicing not insisting on your own way?

_____
_____
_____
_____
_____
_____
_____
_____
_____
_____
_____
_____
_____
_____
_____
_____
_____
_____

DAY 43

Love is…

Not Irritable

"Whoever keeps his mouth and his tongue keeps himself out of trouble." Proverbs 21:23

What is being irritable?

Write down what being irritable means in your own words, look up the definition, and read 1 Corinthians 13 in several different versions to get a good idea of what you're going to be dealing with this week.

_____
_____
_____
_____
_____
_____
_____
_____
_____
_____
_____
_____
_____
_____
_____

DAY 44

Love is…

Not Irritable

"Be not quick in your spirit to become angry, for anger lodges in the heart of fools." Ecclesiastes 7:9

Why is not being irritable important in regards to love?

_____
_____
_____
_____
_____
_____
_____
_____
_____
_____
_____
_____
_____
_____
_____
_____
_____
_____
_____

DAY 45

Love is...

Not Irritable

"A soft answer turns away wrath, but a harsh word stirs up anger."
Proverbs 15:1

Apply it.

How can you work on not being irritable today?

_____
_____
_____
_____
_____
_____
_____
_____
_____
_____
_____
_____
_____
_____
_____
_____
_____

DAY 46

Love is…

Not Irritable

"If we put bits into the mouths of horses so they obey us, we guide their whole bodies as well. Look at the ships also: though they are so large and driven by strong winds, they are guided by a very small rudder wherever the will of the pilot directs. So also the tongue is a small member, yet it boasts of great things. How great a forest is set ablaze by such a small fire!" James 3:3-5

Spend some time in prayer.

Ask God to give you opportunities to work on not being irritable and to help you be aware when those times come, so you can be intentional. Write down anything that comes to mind.

_____
_____
_____
_____
_____
_____
_____
_____
_____
_____
_____
_____

DAY 47

Love is…

Not Irritable

"A man of quick temper acts foolishly, and a man of evil devices is hated." Proverbs 14:17

Take some time to look up verses about not being irritable. Write them below, and then pick one or two to put on a notecard. Take them with you today, and read or say them whenever you get a chance.

_____
_____
_____
_____
_____
_____
_____
_____
_____
_____
_____
_____
_____
_____
_____
_____
_____
_____
_____

DAY 48

Love is…

Not Irritable

"It is not what goes into the mouth that defiles a person, but what comes out of the mouth; this defiles a person." Matthew 15:11

Challenge:

Hold your tongue when you want to give someone a piece of your mind. Be gentle, even if someone's on your last nerve. Take a deep breath, and instead of lashing out, calmly say something nice. Write about your experience below.

_____
_____
_____
_____
_____
_____
_____
_____
_____
_____
_____
_____
_____
_____
_____

DAY 49

Love is…

Not Irritable

"Remind them to be submissive to rulers and authorities, to be obedient, to be ready for every good work, to speak evil of no one, to avoid quarreling, to be gentle, and to show perfect courtesy to all people." Titus 3:1-2

Reflect.

What have you learned while practicing not being irritable?

_____
_____
_____
_____
_____
_____
_____
_____
_____
_____
_____
_____
_____
_____

DAY 50

Love is…

Not Resentful

"Put on then, as God's chosen ones, holy and beloved, compassionate hearts, kindness, humility, meekness, and patience, bearing with one another and, if one has a complaint against another, forgiving each other; as the Lord has forgiven you, so you also must forgive."
Colossians 3:12-13

What is being resentful?

Write down what being resentful means in your own words, look up the definition, and read 1 Corinthians 13 in several different versions to get a good idea of what you're going to be dealing with this week.

_____
_____
_____
_____
_____
_____
_____
_____
_____
_____
_____
_____

DAY 51

Love is…

Not Resentful

"Do not say, 'I will do to him as he has done to me; I will pay the man back for what he has done.'" Proverbs 24:29

Why is not being resentful important in regards to love?

_____
_____
_____
_____
_____
_____
_____
_____
_____
_____
_____
_____
_____
_____
_____
_____
_____
_____
_____
_____

DAY 52

Love is…

Not Resentful

"And whenever you stand praying, forgive, if you have anything against anyone, so that your Father also who is in heaven may forgive your trespasses." Mark 11:25

Apply it.

How can you work on not being resentful today?

_____
_____
_____
_____
_____
_____
_____
_____
_____
_____
_____
_____
_____
_____
_____

DAY 53

Love is…

Not Resentful

"And if he sins against you seven times in the day, and turns to you seven times and says, 'I repent,' you must forgive him." Luke 17:4

Spend some time in prayer.

Ask God to give you opportunities to work on not being resentful and to help you be aware when those times come, so you can be intentional. Write down anything that comes to mind.

_____
_____
_____
_____
_____
_____
_____
_____
_____
_____
_____
_____
_____
_____
_____

DAY 54

Love is…

Not Resentful

"…And forgive us our debts, as we also have forgiven our debtors."
Matthew 6:12

Take some time to look up verses about not being resentful. Write them below, and then pick one or two to put on a notecard. Take them with you today, and read or say them whenever you get a chance.

_____
_____
_____
_____
_____
_____
_____
_____
_____
_____
_____
_____
_____
_____
_____
_____

DAY 55

Love is…

Not Resentful

"For if you forgive others their trespasses, your heavenly Father will also forgive you, but if you do not forgive others their trespasses, neither will your Father forgive your trespasses." Matthew 6:14-15

Challenge:

Forgive someone who has wronged you, and then ask God to help you let it go. Write about your experience below.

_____
_____
_____
_____
_____
_____
_____
_____
_____
_____
_____
_____
_____
_____
_____
_____

DAY 56

Love is…

Not Resentful

"Beloved, never avenge yourselves, but leave it to the wrath of God, for it is written, 'Vengeance is mine, I will repay, says the Lord.'"
Romans 12:19

Reflect.

What have you learned while practicing not being resentful?

_____
_____
_____
_____
_____
_____
_____
_____
_____
_____
_____
_____
_____
_____
_____

DAY 57

Love is…

Joyful in Truth

"He who justifies the wicked and he who condemns the righteous are both alike; an abomination to the Lord." Proverbs 17:15

What does it mean to be joyful in the truth and not in wrongdoings?

Write down what being joyful in truth means in your own words, look up the definition, and read 1 Corinthians 13 in several different versions to get a good idea of what you're going to be dealing with this week.

_____
_____
_____
_____
_____
_____
_____
_____
_____
_____
_____
_____
_____

DAY 58

Love is…

Joyful in Truth

"Do not rejoice when your enemy falls, and let not your heart be glad when he stumbles." Proverbs 24:17

Why is rejoicing in truth and not in wrongdoings important in regards to love?

_____
_____
_____
_____
_____
_____
_____
_____
_____
_____
_____
_____
_____
_____
_____
_____

DAY 59

Love is…

Joyful in Truth

"You shall do no injustice in court. You shall not be partial to the poor or defer to the great, but in righteousness shall you judge your neighbor." Leviticus 19:15

Apply it.

How can you work on rejoicing in truth today?

_____
_____
_____
_____
_____
_____
_____
_____
_____
_____
_____
_____
_____
_____
_____
_____

DAY 60

Love is…

Joyful in Truth

"Lying lips are an abomination to the Lord, but those who act faithfully are his delight." Proverbs 12:22

Spend some time in prayer.

Ask God to give you opportunities to work on rejoicing in truth and not in wrongdoings, and to help you be aware when those times come, so you can be intentional. Write down anything that comes to mind.

_____
_____
_____
_____
_____
_____
_____
_____
_____
_____
_____
_____
_____
_____
_____

DAY 61

Love is…

Joyful in Truth

"Whoever desires to love life and see good days, let him keep his tongue from evil and his lips from speaking deceit; let him turn away from evil and do good; let him seek peace and pursue it. For the eyes of the Lord are on the righteous, and his ears are open to their prayer. But the face of the Lord is against those who do evil." 1 Peter 3:10-12

Take some time to look up verses about rejoicing in truth. Write them below, and then pick one or two to put on a notecard. Take them with you today, and read or say them whenever you get a chance.

_____
_____
_____
_____
_____
_____
_____
_____
_____
_____
_____
_____

DAY 62

Love is…

Joyful in Truth

"A false balance is an abomination to the Lord, but a just weight is his delight." Proverbs 11:1

Challenge:

Confess truth today. Take your thoughts captive and if you start to give in to negativity or the lies of the enemy, rejoice in knowing that God believes just the opposite about you! Speak out the things God says about you. Write about your experience below.

_____
_____
_____
_____
_____
_____
_____
_____
_____
_____
_____
_____
_____
_____

DAY 63

Love is...

Joyful in Truth

"You shall not pervert justice. You shall not show partiality, and you shall not accept a bribe, for a bribe blinds the eyes of the wise and subverts the cause of the righteous. Justice, and only justice, you shall follow, that you may live and inherit the land that the Lord your God is giving you." Deuteronomy 16:19-20

Reflect.

What have you learned while practicing rejoicing in truth and not in wrongdoings?

_____
_____
_____
_____
_____
_____
_____
_____
_____
_____
_____
_____

DAY 64

Love is…

Bearing All Things

"And let us not grow weary of doing good, for in due season we will reap, if we do not give up." Galatians 6:9

What is bearing all things?

Write down what bearing all things means in your own words, look up the definition, and read 1 Corinthians 13 in several different versions to get a good idea of what you're going to be dealing with this week.

_____
_____
_____
_____
_____
_____
_____
_____
_____
_____
_____
_____
_____
_____
_____

DAY 65

Love is…

Bearing All Things

"He gives power to the faint, and to him who has no might he increases strength." Isaiah 40:29

Why is bearing all things important in regards to love?

_____
_____
_____
_____
_____
_____
_____
_____
_____
_____
_____
_____
_____
_____
_____
_____
_____
_____
_____
_____

DAY 66

Love is…

Bearing All Things

"I can do all things through him who strengthens me."

Philippians 4:13

Apply it.

How can you work on bearing all things today?

_____
_____
_____
_____
_____
_____
_____
_____
_____
_____
_____
_____
_____
_____
_____

DAY 67

Love is…

Bearing All Things

"…Walk in a manner worthy of the calling to which you have been called, with all humility and gentleness, with patience, bearing with one another in love, eager to maintain the unity of the Spirit in the bond of peace." Ephesians 4:1-3

Spend some time in prayer.

Ask God to give you opportunities to work on bearing all things and to help you be aware when those times come, so you can be intentional. Write down anything that comes to mind.

_____
_____
_____
_____
_____
_____
_____
_____
_____
_____
_____

DAY 68

Love is…

Bearing All Things

"But they who wait for the Lord shall renew their strength; they shall mount up with wings like eagles; they shall run and not be weary; they shall walk and not faint." Isaiah 40:31

Take some time to look up verses about bearing all things. Write them below, and then pick one or two to put on a notecard. Take them with you today, and read or say them whenever you get a chance.

_____
_____
_____
_____
_____
_____
_____
_____
_____
_____
_____
_____
_____
_____
_____
_____

DAY 69

Love is…

Bearing All Things

"Trust in the Lord with all your heart, and do not lean on your own understanding. In all your ways, acknowledge him, and he will make straight your paths." Proverbs 3:5-6

Challenge:

Don't give up today – on a project, on a person, on a situation. Big or small, finish what you've started or do something you've been putting off. Write about your experience below.

_____
_____
_____
_____
_____
_____
_____
_____
_____
_____
_____
_____
_____
_____

DAY 70

Love is…

Bearing All Things

"Rejoice in hope, be patient in tribulation, be constant in prayer."

Romans 12:12

Reflect.

What have you learned while practicing bearing all things?

_____
_____
_____
_____
_____
_____
_____
_____
_____
_____
_____
_____
_____
_____
_____
_____
_____
_____
_____

DAY 71

Love is…

Believing All Things

"Be watchful, stand firm in the faith, act like men, be strong."

1 Corinthians 16:13

What is believing all things?

Write down what believing all things means in your own words, look up the definition, and read 1 Corinthians 13 in several different versions to get a good idea of what you're going to be dealing with this week.

_____
_____
_____
_____
_____
_____
_____
_____
_____
_____
_____
_____

DAY 72

Love is…

Believing All Things

"Not that we lord it over your faith, but we work with you for your joy, for you stand firm in your faith." 2 Corinthians 1:24

Why is believing all things important in regards to love?

_____
_____
_____
_____
_____
_____
_____
_____
_____
_____
_____
_____
_____
_____
_____
_____
_____
_____

DAY 73

Love is…

Believing All Things

"In all circumstances take up the shield of faith, with which you can extinguish all the flaming darts of the evil one." Ephesians 6:16

Apply it.

How can you work on believing all things today?

_____
_____
_____
_____
_____
_____
_____
_____
_____
_____
_____
_____
_____
_____
_____
_____
_____
_____

DAY 74

Love is…

Believing All Things

"I have fought the good fight, I have finished the race, I have kept the faith." 2 Timothy 4:7

Spend some time in prayer.

Ask God to give you opportunities to work on believing all things and to help you be aware when those times come, so you can be intentional. Write down anything that comes to mind.

_____
_____
_____
_____
_____
_____
_____
_____
_____
_____
_____
_____
_____
_____
_____
_____

DAY 75

Love is…

Believing All Things

"For we walk by faith, not by sight." 2 Corinthians 5:7

Take some time to look up verses about believing all things. Write them below, and then pick one or two to put on a notecard. Take them with you today, and read or say them whenever you get a chance.

_____
_____
_____
_____
_____
_____
_____
_____
_____
_____
_____
_____
_____
_____
_____
_____
_____
_____
_____
_____

DAY 76

Love is…

Believing All Things

"Jesus said to him, 'Have you believed because you have seen me? Blessed are those who have not seen and yet have believed.'"

John 20:29

Challenge:

Memorize a passage of Scripture (at least three verses) that is relevant to your current circumstance. Challenge yourself and watch your faith grow. Write about your experience below.

_____
_____
_____
_____
_____
_____
_____
_____
_____
_____
_____
_____
_____
_____

DAY 77

Love is…

Believing All Things

"And God, who knows the heart, bore witness to them, by giving them the Holy Spirit just as he did to us, and he made no distinction between us and them, having cleansed their hearts by faith." Acts 15:8-9

Reflect.

What have you learned while practicing believing all things?

_____
_____
_____
_____
_____
_____
_____
_____
_____
_____
_____
_____
_____
_____
_____
_____
_____

DAY 78

Love is…

Hoping All Things

"So that by two unchangeable things, in which it is impossible for God to lie, we who have fled for refuge might have strong encouragement to hold fast to the hope set before us. We have this as a sure and steadfast anchor of the soul, a hope that enters into the inner place behind the curtain." Hebrews 6:8-9

What is hoping all things?

Write down what hoping all things means in your own words, look up the definition, and read 1 Corinthians 13 in several different versions to get a good idea of what you're going to be dealing with this week.

_____
_____
_____
_____
_____
_____
_____
_____
_____
_____
_____
_____

DAY 79

Love is…

Hoping All Things

"For in this hope we were saved. Now hope that is seen is not hope. For who hopes for what he sees? But if we hope for what we do not see, we wait for it with patience." Romans 8:24-25

Why is hoping all things important in regards to love?

_____
_____
_____
_____
_____
_____
_____
_____
_____
_____
_____
_____
_____
_____
_____
_____
_____

DAY 80

Love is…

Hoping All Things

"There is one body and one Spirit – just as you were called to the one hope that belongs to your call." Ephesians 4:4

Apply it.

How can you work on hoping all things today?

_____
_____
_____
_____
_____
_____
_____
_____
_____
_____
_____
_____
_____
_____
_____
_____

DAY 81

Love is…

Hoping All Things

"May the God of hope fill you with all joy and peace in believing, so that by the power of the Holy Spirit you may abound in hope."

Romans 15:13

Spend some time in prayer.

Ask God to give you opportunities to work on hoping all things and to help you be aware when those times come, so you can be intentional. Write down anything that comes to mind.

_____
_____
_____
_____
_____
_____
_____
_____
_____
_____
_____
_____
_____

DAY 82

Love is…

Hoping All Things

"Why are you cast down, O my soul, and why are you in turmoil within me? Hope in God; for I shall again praise him, my salvation and my God." Psalm 43:5

Take some time to look up verses about hoping all things. Write them below, and then pick one or two to put on a notecard. Take them with you today, and read or say them whenever you get a chance.

_____
_____
_____
_____
_____
_____
_____
_____
_____
_____
_____
_____
_____
_____
_____

DAY 83

Love is…

Hoping All Things

"Not only that, but we rejoice in our sufferings, knowing that suffering produces endurance, and endurance produces character, and character produces hope, and hope does not put us to shame, because God's love has been poured into our hearts through the Holy Spirit who has been given to us." Romans 5:3-5

Challenge:

Practice positivity. Try not to say, "I can't" this week. Write about your experience below.

_____
_____
_____
_____
_____
_____
_____
_____
_____
_____
_____
_____
_____

DAY 84

Love is…

Hoping All Things

"And now, O Lord, for what do I wait? My hope is in you."

Psalm 39:7

Reflect.

What have you learned while practicing hoping all things?

_____
_____
_____
_____
_____
_____
_____
_____
_____
_____
_____
_____
_____
_____
_____
_____
_____

DAY 85

Love is…

Enduring All Things

"But the one who endures to the end will be saved." Matthew 24:13

What is enduring all things?

Write down what enduring all things means in your own words, look up the definition, and read 1 Corinthians 13 in several different versions to get a good idea of what you're going to be dealing with this week.

_____
_____
_____
_____
_____
_____
_____
_____
_____
_____
_____
_____
_____
_____

DAY 86

Love is…

Enduring All Things

"Therefore, since we are surrounded by so great a cloud of witnesses, let us also lay aside every weight, and sin which clings so closely, and let us run with endurance the race that is set before us, looking to Jesus, the founder and perfecter of our faith, who for the joy that was set before Him endured the cross, despising the shame, and is seated at the right hand of the throne of God." Hebrews 12:1-2

Why is enduring all things important in regards to love?

_____
_____
_____
_____
_____
_____
_____
_____
_____
_____
_____
_____
_____
_____
_____

DAY 87

Love is…

Enduring All Things

"For you know that the testing of your faith produces steadfastness."

James 1:3

Apply it.

How can you work on enduring all things today?

_____
_____
_____
_____
_____
_____
_____
_____
_____
_____
_____
_____
_____
_____
_____

DAY 88

Love is…

Enduring All Things

"Share in suffering as a good soldier of Christ Jesus." 2 Timothy 2:3

Spend some time in prayer.

Ask God to give you opportunities to work on enduring all things and to help you be aware when those times come, so you can be intentional. Write down anything that comes to mind.

_____
_____
_____
_____
_____
_____
_____
_____
_____
_____
_____
_____
_____
_____
_____
_____

DAY 89

Love is…

Enduring All Things

"Rejoice always, pray without ceasing, give thanks in all circumstances; for this is the will of God in Christ Jesus for you."

1 Thessalonians 5:16-18

Take some time to look up verses about enduring all things. Write them below, and then pick one or two to put on a notecard. Take them with you today, and read or say them whenever you get a chance.

_____
_____
_____
_____
_____
_____
_____
_____
_____
_____
_____
_____
_____
_____
_____
_____

DAY 90

Love is…

Enduring All Things

"For you have need of endurance, so that when you have done the will of God you may receive what is promised." Hebrews 10:36

Challenge:

Whatever struggle you are facing right now, do not give up. Tell someone about it and have them pray with you. Surround yourself with God's promises of overcoming. Write about your experience below.

_____
_____
_____
_____
_____
_____
_____
_____
_____
_____
_____
_____
_____
_____
_____

DAY 91

Love is...

Enduring All Things

"In this you rejoice, though now for a little while, if necessary, you have been grieved by various trials, so that the tested genuineness of your faith – more precious than gold that perishes though it is tested by fire – may be found to result in praise and glory and honor at the revelation of Jesus Christ." 1 Peter 1:6-7

Reflect.

What have you learned while practicing enduring all things?

_____
_____
_____
_____
_____
_____
_____
_____
_____
_____
_____
_____
_____

To continue our journey…

Look back on the past thirteen weeks. What has changed? What have you learned? What can you keep with you as you continue to live a life of love?

_____
_____
_____
_____
_____
_____
_____
_____
_____
_____
_____
_____
_____
_____
_____
_____
_____
_____
_____
_____
_____
_____